Pause.

First published 2020
Author & Photographer: Anson H.
ISBN: 9798647291820

With Special Thanks to Angela Cheung.,
who has wholeheartedly encouraged me
to publish this book.

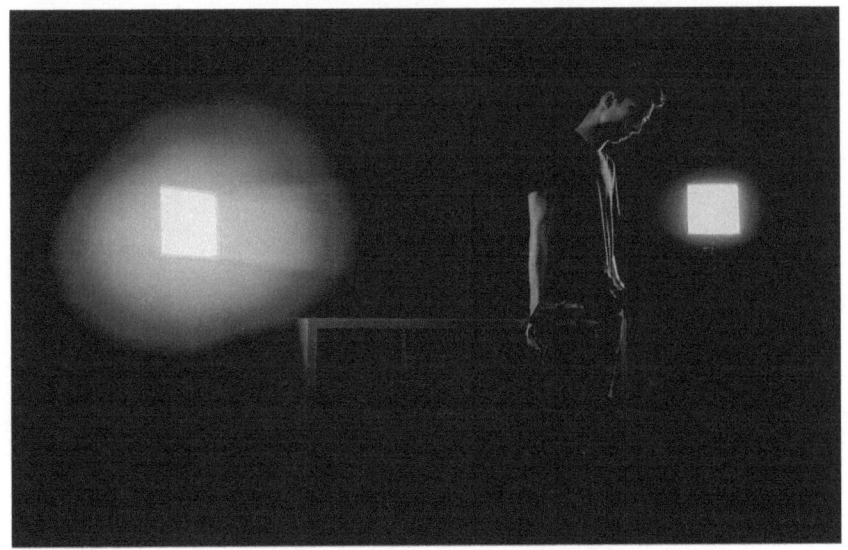

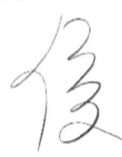

Dedicated to people who just need a break (pause) from their busy lives.

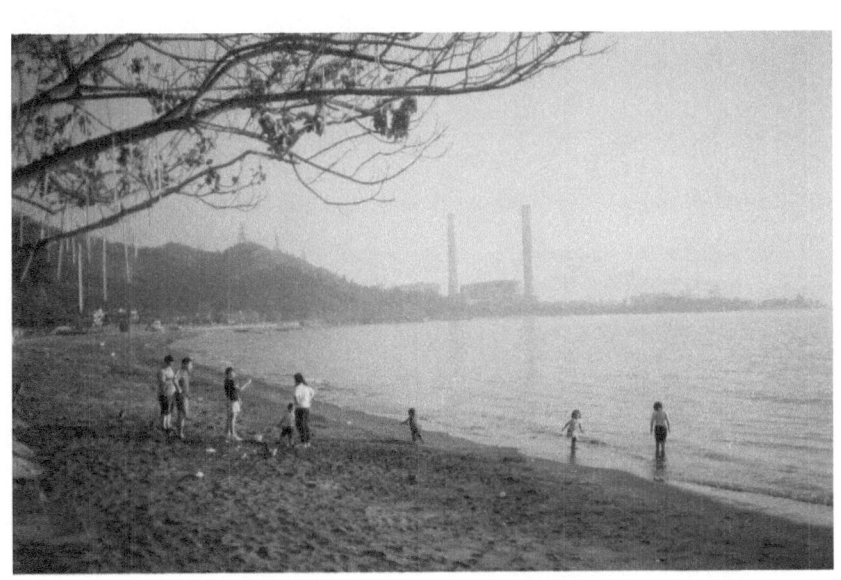

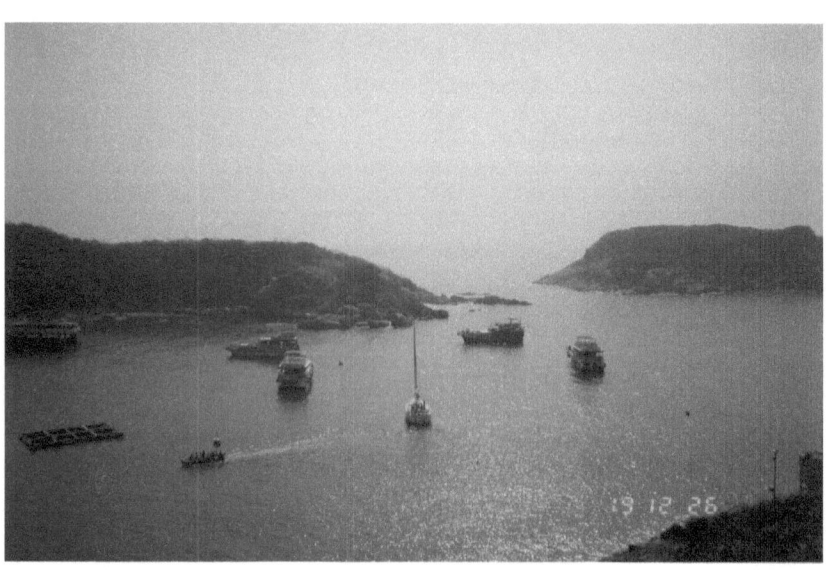

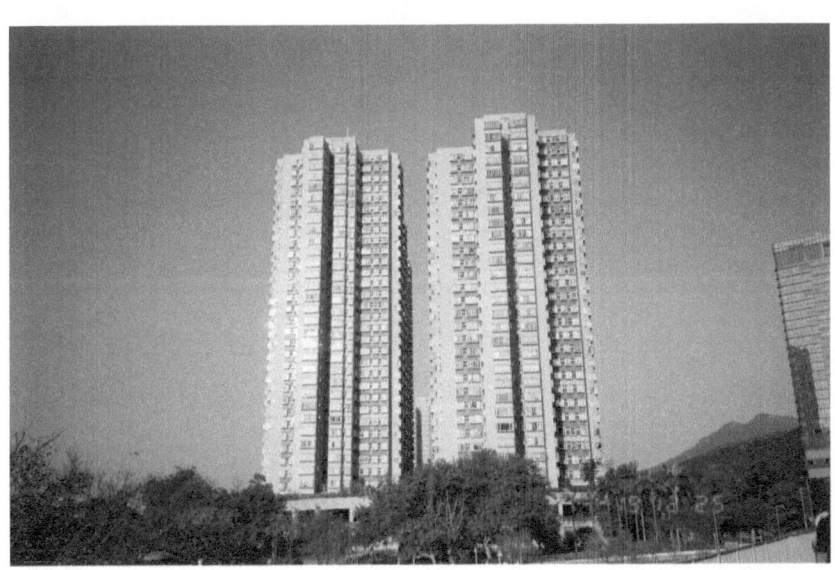

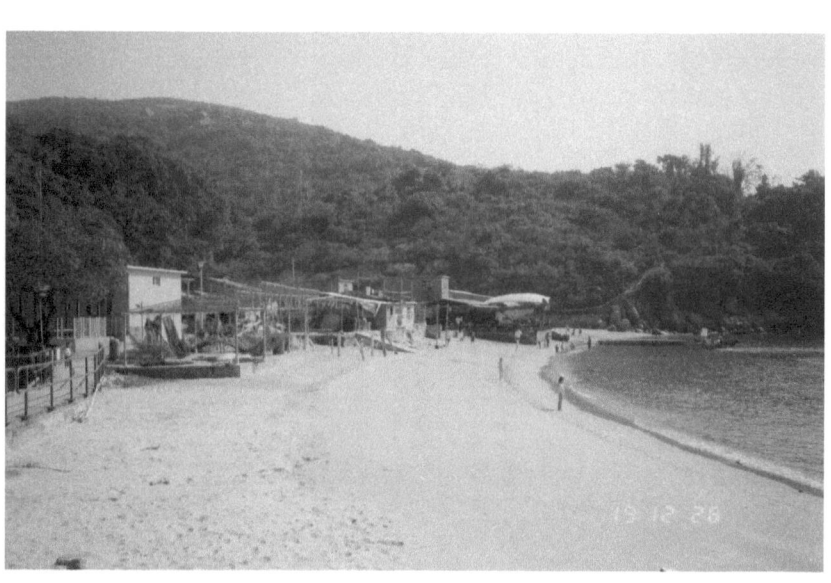

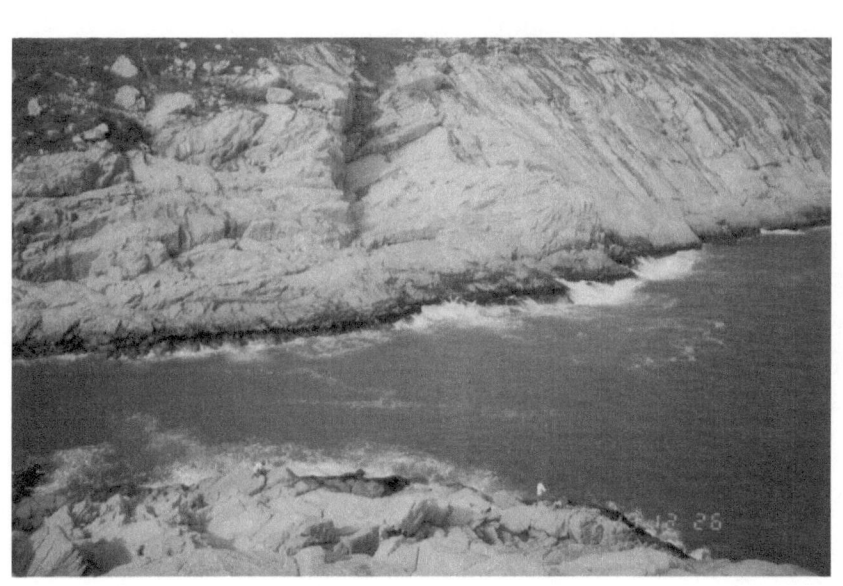

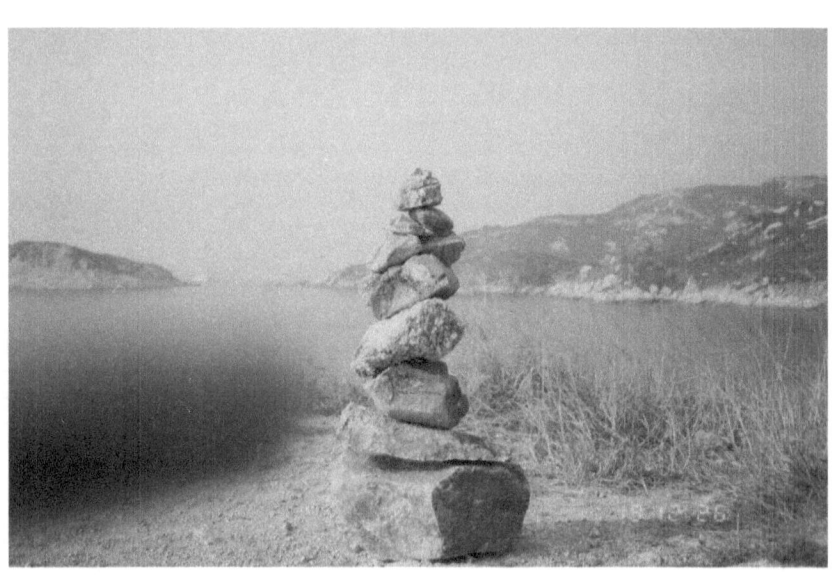

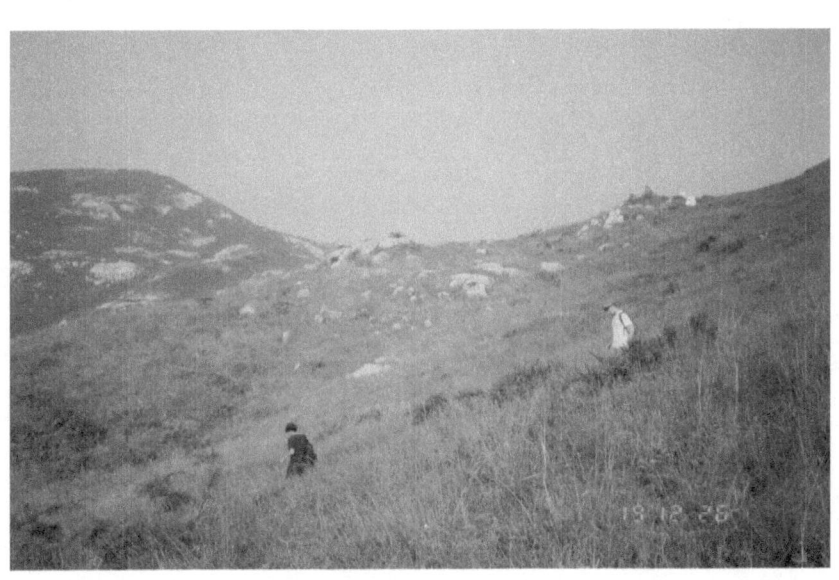

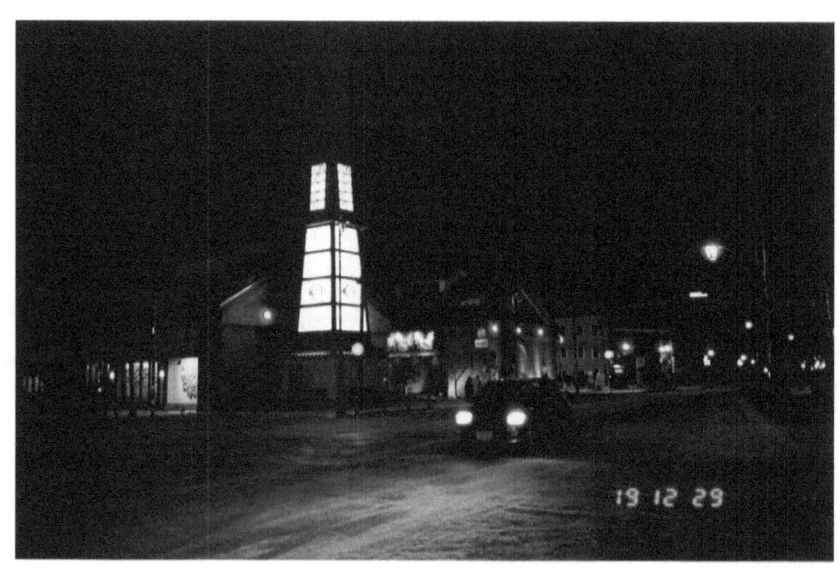

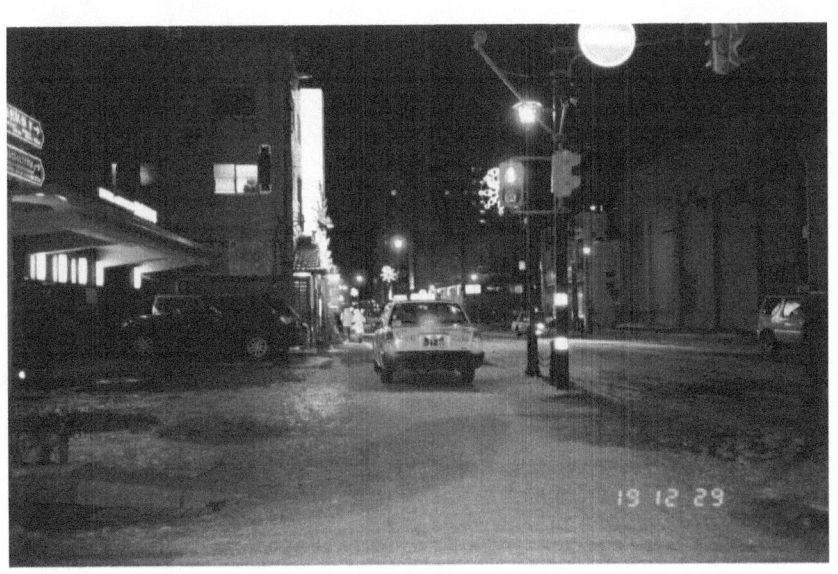

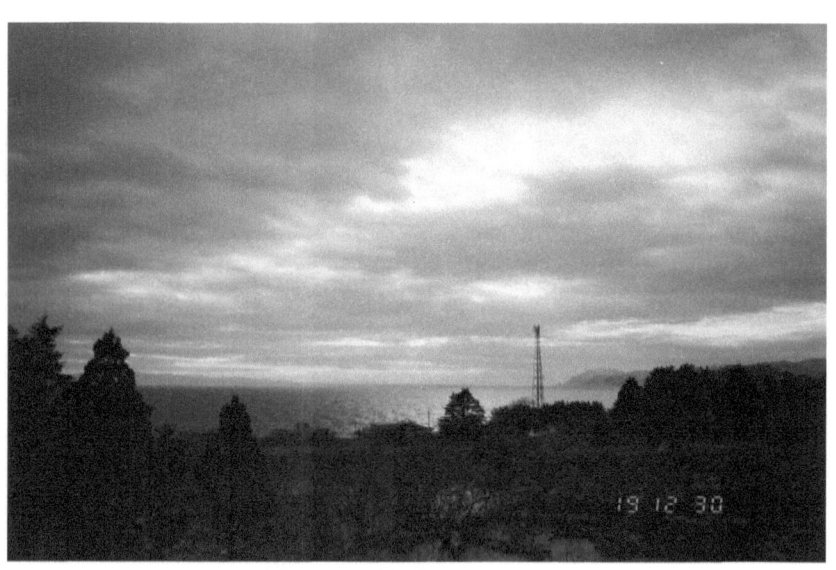

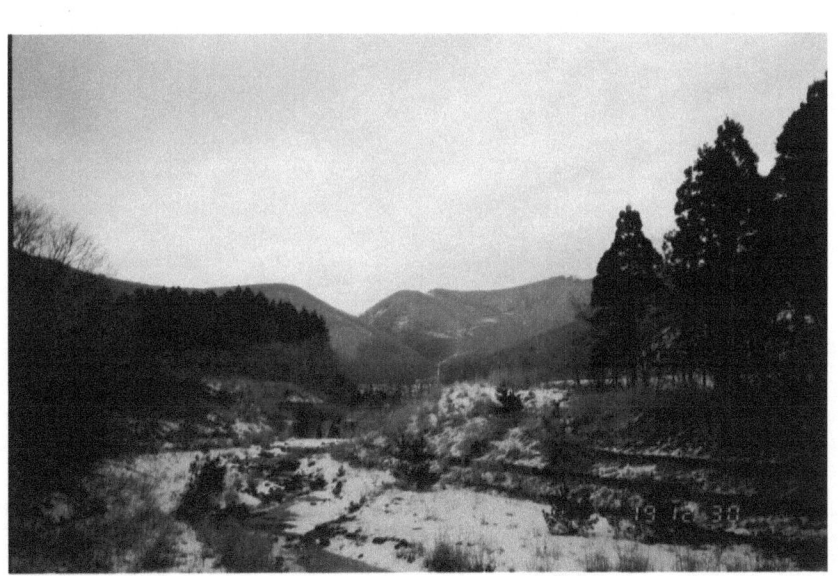

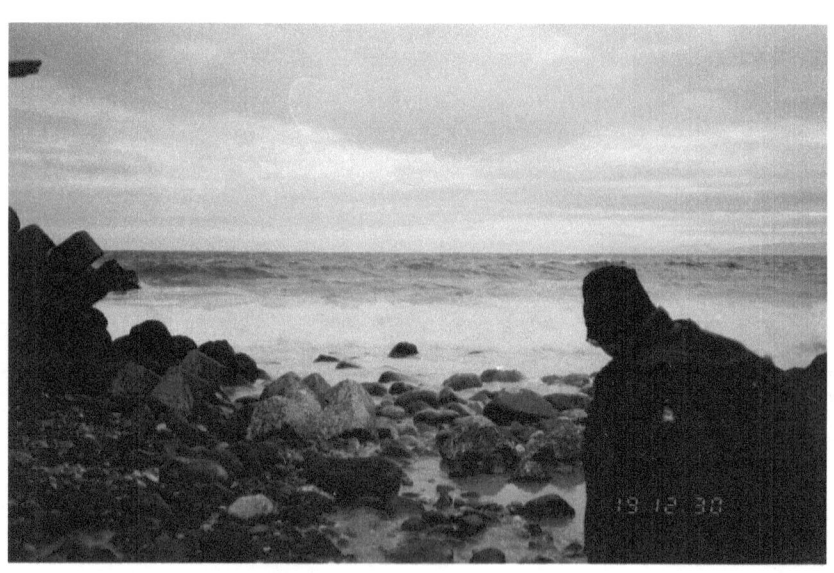

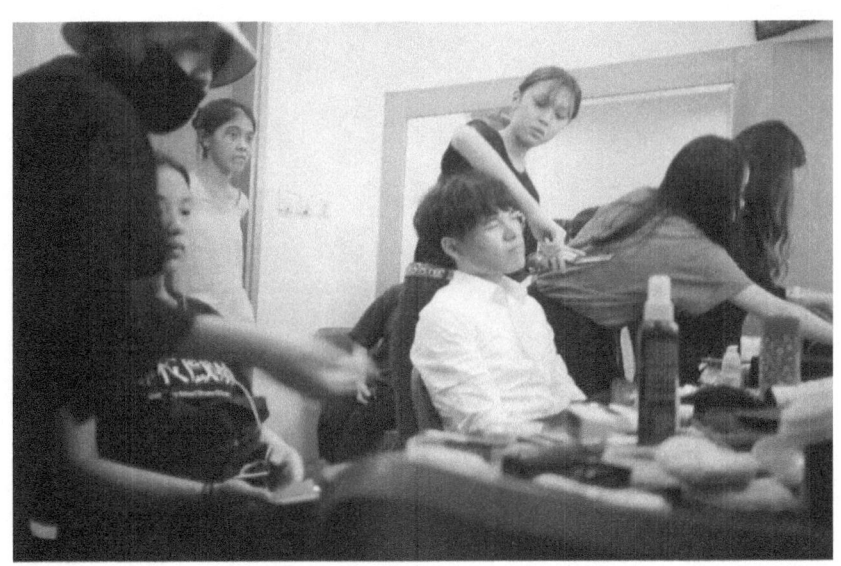

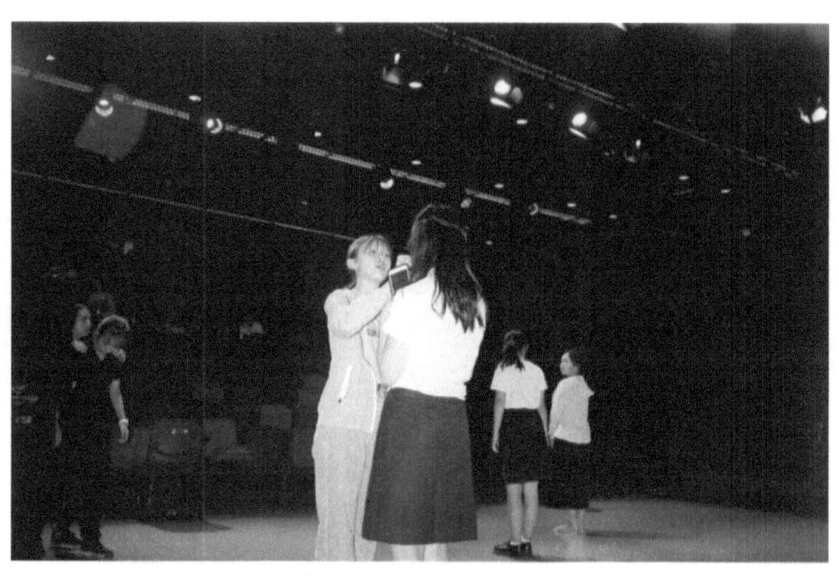

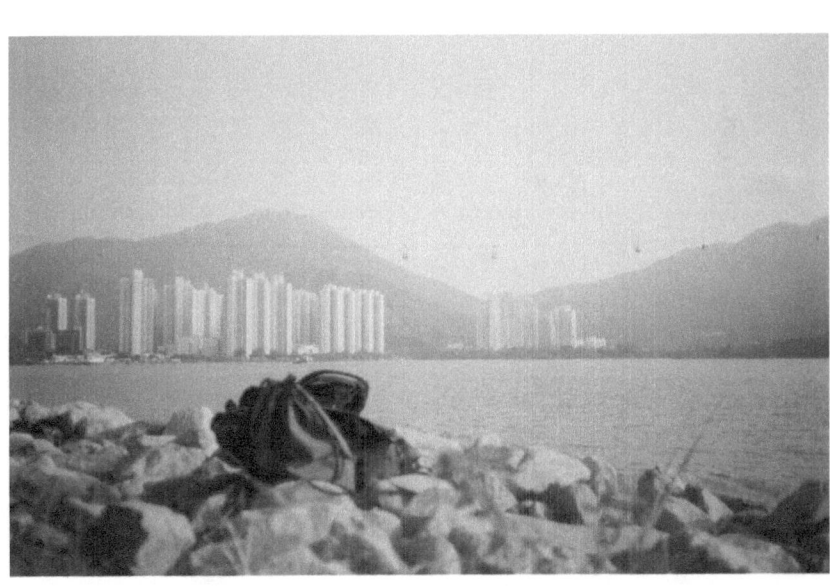

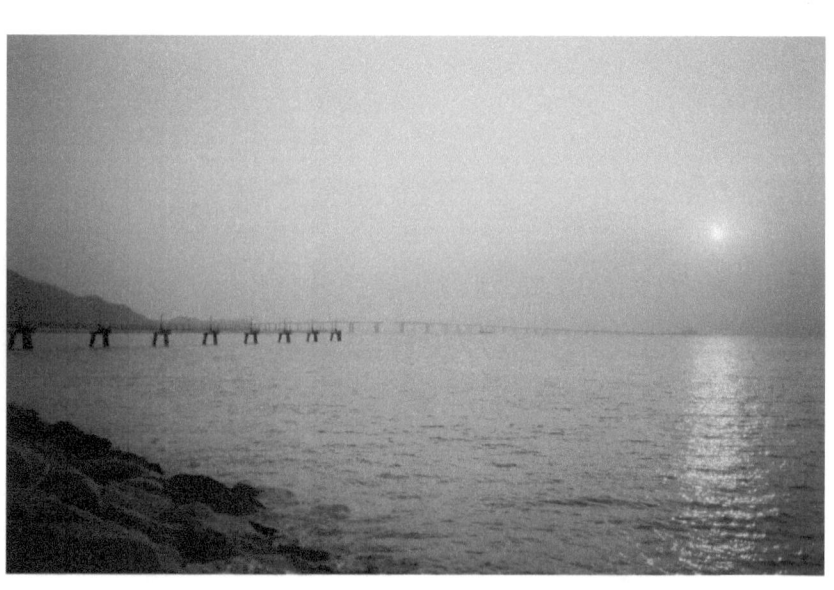

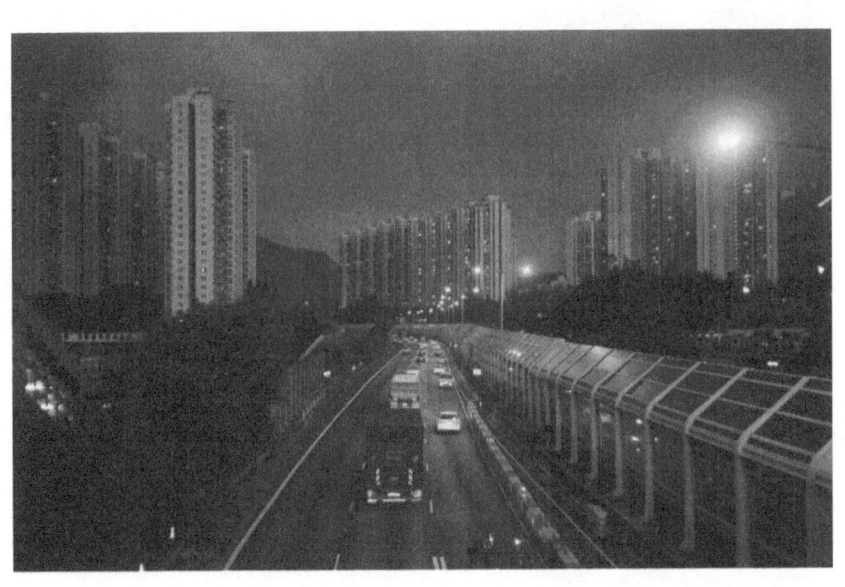

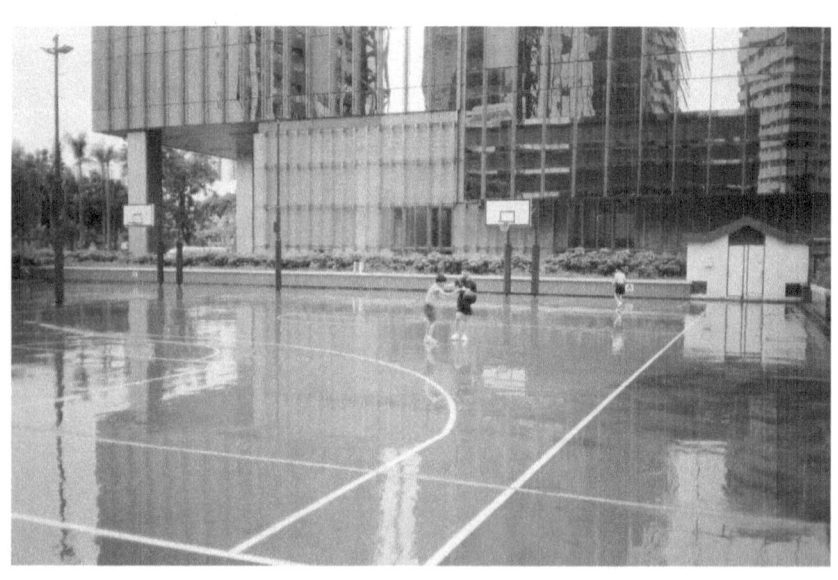

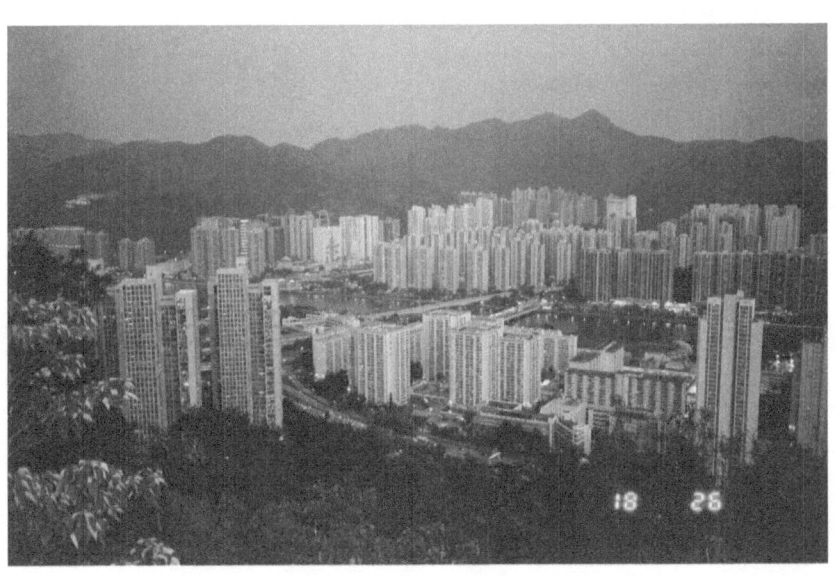

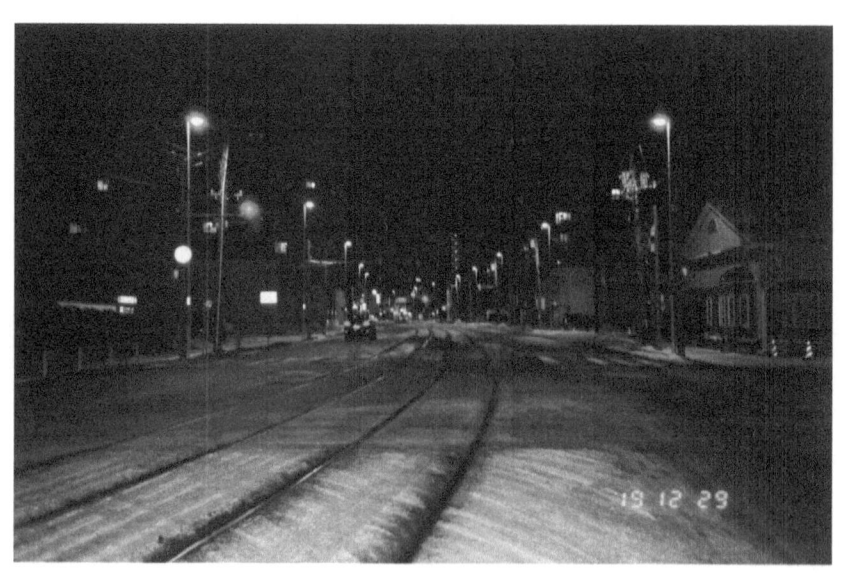

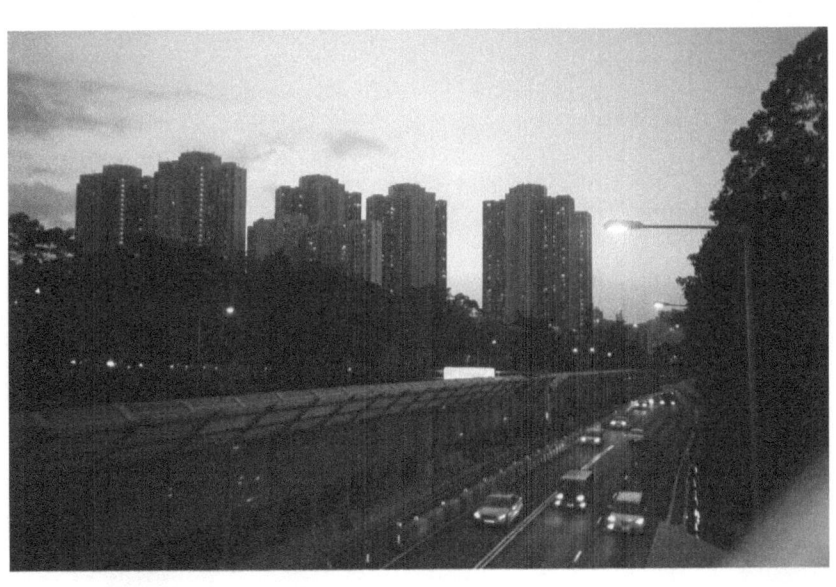

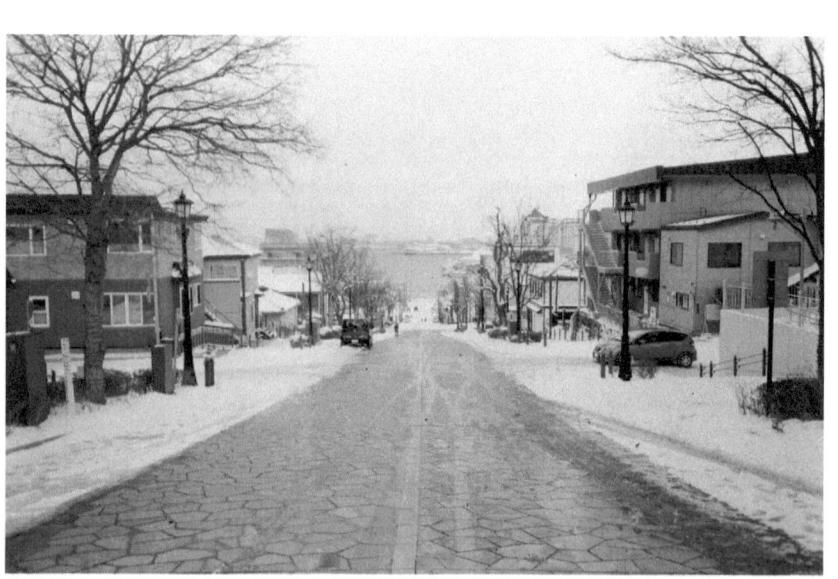

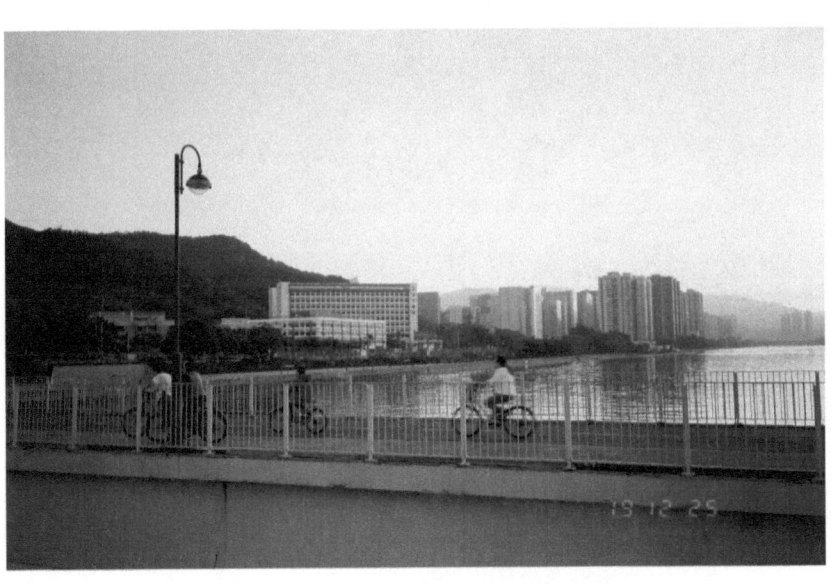

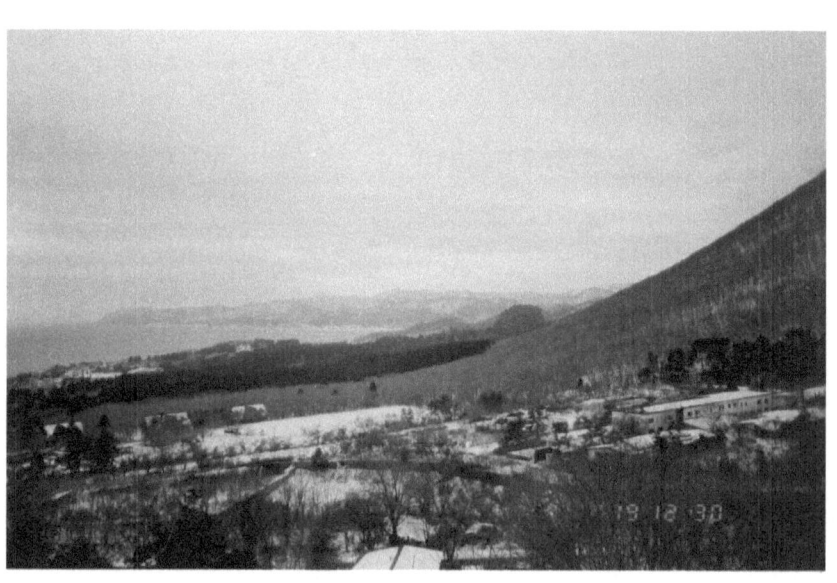